"In a new digital world where instant communication has left us feeling more disconnected than ever, it is the tried and tested values and principles that really make the difference to today's managers. There's a reason why guys like Sam Walton and Lou Pritchett have been so successful. We should all be so lucky as to listen and find out why."

—Dan Mangru,
Host of The Mangru Report on Fox Business

"What the Internet Can't Teach You has, in one place, the lessons one learns in a military career. I know many military people who failed because they didn't learn these principles of leadership and management!"

—Col. Will Merrill,
West Point, Class of 1958, Airborne Ranger, US Army (ret)

"I wish I had had Lou's book back in 1986 when we introduced Stainmaster carpeting to the world. His succinct maxims are a timeless road map to business success, cutting through the fog of circumstance and technology. I recommend it to all young aspiring leaders."

—Tom McAndrews, the "Father of Stainmaster,"
Former DuPont Worldwide Director, Flooring Systems

WHAT THE INTERNET CAN'T TEACH YOU

Ageless Information for the Information Age

LOU PRITCHETT

iUniverse, Inc.
Bloomington

What the Internet Can't Teach You
Ageless Information for the Information Age

iUniverse books may be ordered through booksellers or by contacting:

iUniverse
1663 Liberty Drive
Bloomington, IN 47403
www.iuniverse.com
1-800-Authors (1-800-288-4677)

ISBN: 978-1-4502-9622-9 (pbk)
ISBN: 978-1-4502-9623-6 (cloth)
ISBN: 978-1-4502-9624-3 (ebk)

Printed in the United States of America

iUniverse rev. date: 2/17/2011

To Margie and Frank McComas
for always being there when needed by both dogs and
humans. And to my scoutmaster, Robert L. (Buddy) Irwin
Jr., who taught me that life is always a self-help game.

CONTENTS

FOREWORD

In his new book, *What The Internet Can't Teach You,* Lou Pritchett delivers powerful teachings on change, people, and customers.

Lou Pritchett has been dealing with *people, customers,* and *change* for more than sixty-five years—thirty-six of those years as a sales executive for Procter & Gamble. Although he is reluctant to call himself an expert on dealing with change, people, and customers, his associates, customers, clients, and friends call him a change agent and a human engineer.

People: Lou began to understand the importance of working with other people in a cooperative, non-confrontational mode when he joined the Boy Scouts at the age of twelve. It was in these formative years that he began to realize that the best way to get what he wanted was to help others get what they wanted. Additionally, he realized that the quality of an organization—whether it's the Boy Scouts or, as he realized later in life, a corporation—is determined by the quality, training, dedication, and commitment of the people who make up that organization.

Customers: Lou started dealing with customers when he was ten years old, shining shoes on the streets of Memphis to help with his family's finances. He distinctly remembers trying to find ways to earn more than the going rate of ten cents a shine by providing his customers with a little something extra, or to put it into today's jargon, by adding value. He began by offering to replace worn shoelaces and eventually offered to deliver shoes in need of repair to a cobbler if a customer would drop them by his stand.

Change: Lou saw the magnitude of change firsthand while observing his father's belting business rapidly going the way of buggy whips as small electrical motors replaced the old single drive "belt" system in American industry. On trips with his father to cotton gins throughout the deep South, he heard gin owners tell his father that they were installing "new technology" that would replace the old systems around which his father had built a living. When Lou was twelve years old, he experienced real change when his father died suddenly, the business vanished, and he, his mother, and his sister were left to go it alone.

All management is the management of people, not the management of things. This is unquestionably Lou's most strongly held belief. Managers who value people—human resources—above capital resources will invariably win the most hotly contested competitive battles, especially in the new global economy where raw materials and technology will be available to all. Lou strongly believes that it is ultimately people who offer a competitive advantage.

We are all customers, and we know what we want. We want the organizations we deal with to listen to our problems and to help us find solutions. And, we want to be treated fairly in the process. It became obvious to Lou early in his career that if he could first understand his customer's needs and then meet and exceed those needs, he would have a customer for life—regardless of whether he was selling shoe shines, shoes, or soap.

Lou's years of business experience have convinced him that change is inevitable and should be welcomed, even embraced enthusiastically. Change can threaten a company or whole industry—or it can serve as a fantastic opportunity. It all depends on how individuals and organizations approach it.

Today, Lou believes that change is not only inevitable but that it presents the single greatest opportunity for competitive advantage for leaders, organizations, and industries that deeply understand it, embrace it, and capitalize on it by helping both employees and customers adapt.

This book, although it has value for every senior executive, was not written with them in mind. Rather, it was written for the millions of small business owners, managers, and workers who get up every morning and head off to work with the single-minded determination to do the very best job they are capable of doing in order to grow their businesses.

The small business segment is where the majority of Americans work. It includes entrepreneurs, real estate agents, restaurant owners, travel agents, building contractors, pharmacists, clerks, sales reps, and doctors. They all have one thing in common—they want to better understand the sea change swirling around them and to learn how to turn this change into a positive thing for themselves and their organizations.

For the large majority of these millions of potential American readers and hundreds of millions in the rest of the world, most learning is through osmosis—on the job, through trial and error, through association with other employees, suppliers, and customers, and through reading books and articles that they believe will help them.

The millions of men and women who work in small businesses, many in organizations with fewer than twenty employees, have little need for reengineering or restructuring; rather, their need is for principles and knowledge from credible individuals who have learned and who can distill and communicate their learning and experiences in a meaningful way.

Lou Pritchett's book meets this need in a forceful, credible, memorable way, not by telling the reader how to do something but by sharing ageless information that he and other successful people have learned through trial and error over the years.

Jim Harris
Nationally Syndicated Columnist, *National Post*
Bestselling author of:
The Learning Paradox
and
Blindsided! How to Spot the Next Breakthrough That Will Change Your Business Forever
www.jimharris.com

ACKNOWLEDGMENTS

As I stated in my first book, *Stop Paddling & Start Rocking the Boat,* writing a book is never done single-handedly. This book would never have seen the light of day had it not been for three people: my wife, Barbara Burnette Pritchett , my son, Dr. Bradley L. Pritchett, and my friend Prakash Idnani. Wife Barbara kept reminding me that my days were growing short and if I was ever going to get all the "stuff" I had written and saved over the years into print, I had better get a move on.

Given this challenge from the girl to whom I have been married for fifty-six years, I asked my son Brad if he would help me organize the material. It seemed to me an impossible task to take over forty years of notes, many cryptic, and put the information into any kind of order that a stranger could read and comprehend. Brad not only organized the material but suggested that the concept of the book should be "nuggets of wisdom," which capitalizes on Plato's teaching that "learning is remembering what you already know." We concluded therefore that our book's audience should include experienced managers who need to be reminded of what they already know, and younger people, just entering the business world, who could gain a leg up in the age-old trial-and-error learning process.

Then my good friend Prakash Idnani entered the scene. With his determination and attitude we made this book happen.

To these three people, I am forever indebted for their foresight, encouragement, determination, and willingness to spend the time and effort to make the book a reality.

Lou Pritchett, Ponte Vedra Beach, Florida

Caution: It is not what you read in this book today that's important; rather it is what you do with it tomorrow.

Photo Credit: Rob Kaufman

INTRODUCTION

When I retired from my position as vice-president of sales and customer development for the Procter & Gamble Company in June 1989, I was fifty-seven years old and, according to my friend, Sam Walton, the founder of Wal-Mart, I was simply too young to stop working. Sam was very concerned about the inroads the Japanese had made into the US auto and electronic fields and told me that if someone didn't wake American businesses up, we would all be flipping hamburgers and scrambling to learn Japanese.

Sam challenged me with this task since he knew that I had been somewhat of a maverick at P&G, trying to alert this 152-year-old company (founded in 1837) to the need for dramatic change in the early years of the "information revolution." My message during those hectic days had been "let's learn to partner with our customers instead of simply following the traditional 'we sell, you buy' practice."

Procter & Gamble had been tremendously successful for decades by focusing on the end-using consumer, but it had historically viewed the customer, (the wholesaler, the grocer, the discount stores) as simply middlemen in the supply chain with little influence on the end-using consumer. This may have been somewhat true in the past but currently the product supply and marketing game was rapidly changing and those customers were no longer 'simply middlemen'—they were becoming major league players in the new game.

In fact, the balance of power was rapidly shifting away from the manufacturers and to the wholesale and retail customers; if we didn't recognize this shift early on and do something about it, we just might lose all we had gained during the past few years. I believed that if we could "cut the template" for the rules of this new game, we would gain the tremendous momentum afforded by an early start. If we could be first and set the ground rules, then we would be in a position to influence the development of this exciting new world of information technology and its impact on our industry. We could become the leader of the revolution, not just another follower. This was powerful, heady stuff for me, a guy who was overconfident in his convictions and his ability to sell them to anyone who would listen and who believed sincerely that if change in P&G was to occur, I had to be one of the agents of that change.

Sam and I first met on a now-famous canoe trip down the South Fork of the Spring River in Northeast Arkansas in 1987, and we agreed that we needed to change the game. (For those interested, this tale is told in great detail in my book, *Stop Paddling & Start Rocking the Boat*, 1995, Harper Collins, and in Sam Walton's book, *Made in America*, 1992, Doubleday.) While Sam and I may be credited as the architects of the partnership that changed the way America does business, it was scores of intelligent, dedicated P&G and Wal-Mart people who really did the grunt work and made it happen. Today, over two decades later, because of P&G's lead with Wal-Mart, collaboration between supplier and customer to better serve the end-using consumer has positively transformed the entire grocery industry. The P&G/Wal-Mart partnership truly became the gold standard for thousands of businesses worldwide. (See Harvard Business School Case Study #9-907-011, *Lou Pritchett: Negotiating the P&G Relationship with Wal-Mart*, January 16, 2007.)

So, back in 1989, even after retirement, I could not get Sam's admonition about giving America a wake-up call out of my mind. Then, out of the blue, I was contacted by Les Tuerk, a top executive from the Leigh Bureau, a premier speakers bureau in New York. Les asked if I had any interest in giving public speaking a try, and I immediately realized that this was the wake-up call opportunity that Sam and I had discussed. I immediately signed on as an exclusive Leigh Bureau speaker, and, on September 13, 1989, only one week after signing, I was telling a hundred employees of State Street Bank in Boston that if they did not immediately recognize the rapid changes in marketing brought about by the "great enabler," the microchip, they were in grave danger of being denied entry into the new game that was beginning to be played.

Rapidly on the heels of the State Street Bank speech, I found myself on a roll, with four or five speaking engagements each month, month after month. Not only was I delivering presentations to US companies, I was also speaking to corporations and associations in France, Belgium, Italy, Japan, China, Mexico, Argentina, Australia, and the UK.

Following many of these presentations, there were question-and-answer sessions. Members of the audience would ask questions about anything I had said. They frequently asked what I thought about various other issues as well. After my first few months on stage, it became obvious that the most-asked question was what advice I could offer for competing in this rapidly developing world that was driven by information technology. Audiences voiced a real concern that what they had done only yesterday was often outdated today—and they wanted to hear what guidelines, principles, rules, maybe even "wisdom" this old guy could give them to help them compete.

I was in the Louvre Museum Conference Center in Paris when my translator relayed a question to me that started me thinking about this book. The question was, "Mr. Pritchett, given your forty-years' experience in business, can you provide us with some sort of list of the most important things you have learned during your career? My colleagues and I aren't getting this on the Internet." On the long flight home from Paris, I decided to begin compiling those bits and pieces of wisdom and universal truth that I had learned from my superiors, my peers, my subordinates, my customers, my suppliers, my teachers, and many, many authors over the previous four decades.

That single question made me realize that the stored intellectual property or wisdom that today's "pre-Internet" managers possess will retire with them. So the question becomes, how do we capture that information, how do we preserve it, and how do we teach it and share it so that the next generations benefit? That was the genesis of this book.

According to Plato, learning is remembering what you already know. Therefore, I am hopeful that the following teachings will help readers remember, and thus learn from, this ageless information that just might not be available on the Internet.

Photo: Collection of the author

On Management

Management: (From Old French ménagement, the art of conducting, directing; from Latin manu agere, to lead by the hand) characterizes the process of leading and directing all or part of an organization, often a business, through the deployment and manipulation of resources (human, financial, material, intellectual, or intangible).

Each morning, millions of managers, from supervisors at McDonalds to Fortune 500 presidents, get up, shave their faces or apply their makeup, and go to their respective jobs—desperately wanting to succeed but becoming totally frustrated. Why? Quite simply because they realize that the old system of mentoring, storytelling, and face-to-face discussions is rapidly vanishing and they desperately miss the days where learning via listening and dialogue was standard procedure.

This book targets the American manager, construed in the broadest sense as any of the millions of entrepreneurs, educators, real estate agents, executives, restaurant owners, travel agents, secretaries, building contractors, druggists, clerks, sales reps, doctors, and anyone else whose job requires them to work with and train people. All share a common goal of getting the best out of their suppliers, coworkers, and employees, but these millions of men and women are finding that the Internet is no substitute for face-to-face dialogue. Instead, they realize that all of the marvelous high-speed technology that is available at their fingertips is a far cry from the touch of a mentor or a boss or a friend who sits with them and works through the issues.

For more than ten years, I searched for a book, any book, that would lay out the pitfalls of the almighty Internet and its beguiling ability to subtly replace one-on-one personal contact and learning. I discovered hundreds, perhaps thousands, of books and articles on everything, including how to manage, how to lead, how to train, how to transform, how to reengineer, how to motivate, how to downsize, how to grow, how to inspire, how to market. I found no lack of good material written by smart people on every subject even remotely associated with the theory of managing and leading both large and small business enterprises.

Astonishingly, I also discovered that there were no books that called attention to the dangers of this new and mind-boggling thing called the Internet replacing the human touch, oral tradition, human passion, and the atavistic pulse within us all that asks, "how may I serve you?" Nor were there any books that summarized the personal and institutional learning of the millions of men and women who had gone before—no one had summarized this ageless information into a simple, easy-to-comprehend guide.

The Internet, for all its wonderful positives, had once again demonstrated the wisdom of the old Jesuit saying, "Your greatest strength, faithfully carried out, can eventually become a weakness." Loosely paraphrased, I believe that the Internet has moved many to use electronic communication only, leaving a frigid void in old-school interpersonal communications where we learned through caring, sharing, and human-to-human dialogue. We are rapidly losing the one-on-one, the storytelling process that the cultures before us so successfully used to transfer rules, mores, acceptable behavior, taboos, etc. to those who would follow. Text messaging, (thumb-to-thumb communication, as my good friend Forrest Cottrell calls it), and e-mailing, as fast and expedient as they are, are no substitutes for face-to-face dialogue and even confrontation.

It is now my hope that this book will accomplish two goals: first, I hope it will share with today's managers some of the ageless wisdom hammered out by those who have gone before; and second, I hope it will sensitize those managers who, today, are trying to survive in this take-no-prisoners environment, to the pitfalls of assigning all of their communications to the computer, for a false god it may be.

"ALL WISDOM IS PLAGIARISM. ONLY STUPIDITY IS ORIGINAL."

HUGH KERR

ALL MANAGEMENT IS THE MANAGEMENT
OF PEOPLE NOT OF THINGS.

"GOOD MANAGEMENT
CONSISTS IN SHOWING
AVERAGE PEOPLE HOW
TO DO THE WORK OF
SUPERIOR PEOPLE."

JOHN D. ROCKEFELLER

When asked to list specifically what resources they manage, most managers name products, machinery, buildings, land, and trucks. Most never mention their key and most expensive resource: people.

"Fish discover water last."

Taoist saying

MANAGERS MUST BE CUSTOMER-
DRIVEN NOT PRODUCT-DRIVEN.
BY DESIGN, A PRODUCT-DRIVEN
COMPANY IS INTERNALLY FOCUSED
WHEREAS A CUSTOMER-DRIVEN
COMPANY IS EXTERNALLY FOCUSED.

"BUSINESS IS NOT JUST DOING DEALS; BUSINESS IS HAVING GREAT PRODUCTS, DOING GREAT ENGINEERING, AND PROVIDING TREMENDOUS SERVICE TO CUSTOMERS. FINALLY, BUSINESS IS A COBWEB OF HUMAN RELATIONSHIPS."

ROSS PEROT

Managers must never fail to tell the truth and must demand that their employees always tell them the truth. Failing to be truthful in any environment is destructive.

"TRUTH IS THE PROPERTY
OF NO INDIVIDUAL
BUT IS THE TREASURE
OF ALL MEN."

RALPH WALDO EMERSON

MANAGERS MUST UNDERSTAND AND
ACCEPT THAT THEY ARE NOT SMARTER
THAN EVERYONE REPORTING TO THEM.
HAVE YOU EVER MET ONE PERSON
WHO WAS SMARTER THAN TEN?

"NONE OF US IS AS SMART AS ALL OF US."

PHIL CONDIT

EMBRACE RATHER THAN RESIST CHANGE. CHANGE IS THE ONLY CONSTANT IN THE UNIVERSE, AND FAILING TO RECOGNIZE THIS FACT IS A LEADING CAUSE OF CORPORATE FAILURES.

"IT'S NOT THE STRONGEST
OF THE SPECIES WHO
SURVIVE, NOR THE MOST
INTELLIGENT, BUT THE
ONES MOST RESPONSIVE
TO CHANGE."

CHARLES DARWIN

UNDERSTAND THAT SERVING THE CUSTOMER IS PARAMOUNT. CUSTOMERS DEMAND CUSTOM, NOT GENERIC, SOLUTIONS TO THEIR PROBLEMS, AND THEY SEEK PRODUCTS THEY TRUST, NOT JUST PRODUCTS THAT MEET A NEED.

"SUPPLIERS HAVE MARKET POWER BECAUSE THEY HAVE INFORMATION ABOUT A PRODUCT OR A SERVICE THAT THE CUSTOMER DOES NOT AND CANNOT HAVE— AND DOES NOT NEED IF HE CAN TRUST THE BRAND."

PETER DRUCKER

Manage risk rather than avoid risk. You will never steal second base with one foot on first.

"THERE ARE RISKS AND COSTS TO A PROGRAM OF ACTION. BUT THEY ARE FAR LESS THAN THE LONG-RANGE RISKS AND COSTS OF COMFORTABLE INACTION."

JOHN F. KENNEDY

IT IS PURE FOLLY WHEN MANAGERS
ATTEMPT TO OVERCOME ANY AND
ALL OBJECTIONS BEFORE TRYING
SOMETHING NEW AND DIFFERENT.

"NOTHING WILL EVER
BE ATTEMPTED IF ALL
POSSIBLE OBJECTIONS
MUST FIRST BE OVERCOME."

NATHAN CUMMINGS

Managers must be able to communicate both vertically and laterally. Some managers are world-class in communicating up and down the organization but find it all but impossible to communicate with their peers and counterparts.

Great leaders all have one trait in common: they are, first, great followers.

MANAGERS HAVE REACHED THE
APEX OF MATURITY WHEN THEY
REALIZE THAT BECOMING A
"BUILDER" IS MORE REWARDING
THAN REMAINING JUST A "FIXER."

THE DEADLY 90-9-1 PARADIGM
90 PERCENT OF MANAGERS SPEND
TODAY THINKING ABOUT YESTERDAY.
9 PERCENT OF MANAGERS SPEND
TODAY THINKING ABOUT TODAY.
BUT ONLY 1 PERCENT OF
MANAGERS SPEND TODAY
THINKING ABOUT TOMORROW.

"THE BEST WAY TO
PREDICT THE FUTURE
IS TO INVENT IT."

ALAN KAY

MANAGERS ARE AWARDED
AUTHORITY FROM THEIR SUPERIORS,
WHILE LEADERS EARN AUTHORITY
FROM THEIR SUBORDINATES. IT
IS LEADERS, THEREFORE, WHO
MAKE THE DIFFERENCE.

MANAGERS MUST NEVER FEAR
CRITICISM; RATHER, THEY MUST
WELCOME IT BECAUSE CRITICISM IS THE
FUEL THAT DRIVES SELF-IMPROVEMENT.

"YOU CAN'T OPERATE
A COMPANY BY FEAR,
BECAUSE THE WAY TO
ELIMINATE FEAR IS TO
AVOID CRITICISM. AND THE
WAY TO AVOID CRITICISM
IS TO DO NOTHING."

STEVE ROSS

ONE OF THE CARDINAL RULES OF BASEBALL IS THAT THE UMPIRE AT THIRD BASE DOESN'T CALL BALLS AND STRIKES AT HOME PLATE. IT'S NOT BECAUSE HE ISN'T QUALIFIED, RATHER IT'S BECAUSE HE IS OUT OF POSITION. WHAT WE SEE DEPENDS UPON WHERE WE STAND, AND THIS PRINCIPLE APPLIES TO MANAGEMENT AS WELL.

THE GREATEST CHALLENGE FOR MANAGEMENT IN THE TWENTY-FIRST CENTURY WILL BE PROBLEM SEEING, NOT PROBLEM SOLVING.

NEVER CREATE AN ENVIRONMENT WHERE SUBORDINATES FEEL THAT THEY MUST TELL YOU WHAT YOU WANT TO HEAR. MANAGEMENT CANNOT PARTICIPATE IN THE PROBLEM-SOLVING PROCESS IF THEY HEAR ONLY THE GOOD NEWS.

"THE PEOPLE TO FEAR ARE NOT THOSE WHO DISAGREE WITH YOU, BUT THOSE WHO DISAGREE WITH YOU AND ARE TOO COWARDLY TO LET YOU KNOW."

NAPOLEON BONAPARTE

MANAGERS MUST NOT CONFUSE
MANAGEMENT AND LEADERSHIP.
MANAGEMENT IS OF DOLLARS
AND THINGS. LEADERSHIP IS OF
HEARTS, SOULS, AND SPIRITS.

"TRUE WISDOM INVOLVES
THE HEAD, THE HEART,
AND THE HAND."

THOMAS BERRY

MANAGERS MUST DEVELOP A SHARED
VISION FOR THE FUTURE—ONE
THAT IS SHARED WITH EMPLOYEES,
SHARED WITH CUSTOMERS, AND
SHARED WITH SUPPLIERS. SHARED
VISIONS ARE ALWAYS WIN-WIN.

"WHERE THERE IS NO
VISION, THE PEOPLE
WILL PERISH."

PROVERBS 29:18

MANAGEMENT MUST BE WILLING TO
PROACTIVELY CHANGE THE RULES
OF THE GAME. PERFECTING A GAME
THAT IS NO LONGER BEING PLAYED
IS EQUIVALENT TO REARRANGING
THE DECK CHAIRS ON THE TITANIC.

"IF YOU DON'T KNOW
WHERE YOU ARE
GOING, ANY ROAD WILL
GET YOU THERE."

LEWIS CARROLL

ALL BUSINESS IS DYNAMIC, NEVER STATIC. THOSE BUSINESSES THAT REMAIN NARROWLY FOCUSED ON DOING THINGS RIGHT, AS OPPOSED TO DOING THE RIGHT THINGS, ARE DOOMED.

"MANAGEMENT IS
DOING THINGS RIGHT;
LEADERSHIP IS DOING
THE RIGHT THINGS."

PETER DRUCKER

GOOD MANAGERS NEVER REPEAT THE SAME ACTION OR PROCESS AND EXPECT DIFFERENT OUTCOMES. INSANITY IS COMMONLY DEFINED AS DOING THE SAME THINGS OVER AND OVER WHILE EXPECTING DIFFERENT RESULTS.

"IF WE ARE TO ACHIEVE RESULTS NEVER BEFORE ACCOMPLISHED, WE MUST EXPECT TO EMPLOY METHODS NEVER BEFORE ATTEMPTED."

FRANCIS BACON

DELEGATE! THE GENIUS OF
MANAGEMENT IS THE ABILITY TO
SKILLFULLY DEPLOY RESOURCES. THIS
MEANS LETTING GO AND ALLOWING
OTHERS TO PARTICIPATE IN THE GAME.

"IF YOU TREAT STAFF AS
YOUR EQUALS, THEY'LL
ROLL THEIR SLEEVES UP
TO GET THE JOB DONE."

JOHN ILHAN

PERMIT MISTAKES! THE VERY BEST COMPANIES HAVE A HIGH TOLERANCE FOR MISTAKES BECAUSE THEY REALIZE THAT WITHOUT THE RISK OF MAKING MISTAKES, INNOVATION IS IMPOSSIBLE. RISK TAKING AND MISTAKE MAKING GO HAND IN HAND.

"WELL, WHEN YOU ARE
TRYING TO CREATE THINGS
THAT ARE NEW, YOU HAVE
TO BE PREPARED TO BE
ON THE EDGE OF RISK."

MICHAEL EISNER

ONE OF THE GREATEST
MISCONCEPTIONS OF MANAGEMENT
IS THE BELIEF THAT FOR THEM
TO WIN OTHERS MUST LOSE.

"I HAVE FOUND NO GREATER SATISFACTION THAN ACHIEVING SUCCESS THROUGH HONEST DEALING AND STRICT ADHERENCE TO THE VIEW THAT, FOR YOU TO GAIN, THOSE YOU DEAL WITH SHOULD GAIN AS WELL."

ALAN GREENSPAN

THERE IS NOT A MANAGER ALIVE
WHO KNOWS ALL THE BUSINESS
ISSUES BETTER THAN THE COMBINED
KNOWLEDGE AND SKILLS OF HIS OR HER
EMPLOYEES AT ALL POSITIONS AND ALL
LEVELS THROUGHOUT THE COMPANY.

PROVIDE CONSTRUCTIVE FEEDBACK,
WHETHER IT BE CRITICISM OR
PRAISE. PROMPT AND HONEST
FEEDBACK IS THE LODESTONE OF
SOUND EMPLOYEE ATTITUDES.

"SANDWICH EVERY BIT OF
CRITICISM BETWEEN TWO
THICK LAYERS OF PRAISE."

MARY KAY ASH

WHEN YOU SHOOT THE MESSENGER,
YOU INSTANTLY STOP RECEIVING
RELIABLE MESSAGES.

"TRUST MEN, AND THEY
WILL BE TRUE TO YOU;
TREAT THEM GREATLY,
AND THEY WILL SHOW
THEMSELVES GREAT."

RALPH WALDO EMERSON

TRUST, AS MUCH AS CAPITAL, IS
A RESOURCE MANDATORY FOR
SYSTEM OPTIMIZATION. TRUST IS
THE UNIVERSAL LANGUAGE FOR
ALL SUCCESSFUL PARTNERSHIPS!
WITHOUT TRUST THERE CAN BE NO
COOPERATION AMONG CUSTOMERS,
SUPPLIERS, TEAMS, DEPARTMENTS,
LABOR, AND MANAGEMENT.

"IF YOU DON'T TRUST
YOUR ASSOCIATES TO
KNOW WHAT IS GOING
ON, THEY'LL KNOW YOU
DON'T REALLY CONSIDER
THEM PARTNERS."

DON SODERQUIST

Many corporate problems stem from management insecurity. What managers should be striving to do is to come to work each day willing to be fired for challenging the system and promoting change. Managers must never surround themselves with Yes-men and women. Creating an environment where your people always agree with you is a prescription for failure. The greatest gift you can give your people is the freedom to speak out and push back. It is a win-win since you will obtain sound advice, and they will receive the satisfaction of contributing.

TO BELIEVE THAT NOTHING WILL WORK AS WELL WITHOUT YOU AS IT WILL WITH YOU IS ARROGANT EGO AT WORK AND IS THE NUMBER ONE CREATIVITY KILLER WITHIN AN ORGANIZATION.

THE MOST EFFECTIVE MANAGERS REALIZE THAT THEY HAVE AVAILABLE (FREE OF CHARGE) THREE HUMAN RESOURCES: SUPERIORS, PEERS, AND SUBORDINATES. THOSE WHO USE ONLY ONE OR TWO ARE DRAMATICALLY SHORTCHANGING THEMSELVES.

MANAGERS MUST BE WILLING TO SHARE INFORMATION WITH SUBORDINATES. THE OLD DAYS OF "NEED TO KNOW," WHERE ALL INFORMATION WAS GUARDED AND HELD CLOSE TO THE CHEST BY MANAGERS WHO FEARED THAT SUBORDINATES COULDN'T HANDLE IT, ARE HISTORY.

"IN THE PAST, A
LEADER WAS A BOSS.
TODAY'S LEADERS
MUST BE PARTNERS
WITH THEIR PEOPLE;
THEY CAN NO LONGER
LEAD SOLELY BASED ON
POSITIONAL POWER."

KEN BLANCHARD

THE MOST EFFECTIVE MANAGERS
NEVER CONFUSE WHAT NEEDS TO BE
DONE WITH WHAT'S NICE TO DO.

WHEN THE BUSINESS POLITICS OF WHO
YOU KNOW BECOME MORE IMPORTANT
THAN WHAT YOU KNOW, PRODUCTIVITY
IS DRAMATICALLY CURTAILED.

IT IS A REFLECTION OF SUPERIOR
LEADERSHIP WHEN PEOPLE PERFORM
ABOVE AND BEYOND BECAUSE THEY
WANT TO, NOT BECAUSE THEY HAVE TO.

"YOU CAN EMPLOY MEN
AND HIRE HANDS TO WORK
FOR YOU, BUT YOU MUST
WIN THEIR HEARTS TO HAVE
THEM WORK WITH YOU."

TIORIO

LISTEN AND LEARN FROM PEOPLE
MANY LEVELS BELOW YOU IN THE
ORGANIZATION; THE PEOPLE NEAR THE
BOTTOM OF THE ORGANIZATION KNOW
PRECISELY WHERE THE PROBLEMS LIE
AND WILL GLADLY TELL YOU IF YOU
BUT ASK AND ALLOW THEM TO.

"WHEN YOU CONFRONT
A PROBLEM YOU BEGIN
TO SOLVE IT."

RUDY GIULIANI

To learn how to manage you must first learn how not to manage.

It's not what you don't know that hurts you; it's what you do know that isn't true.

There is a night-and-day difference between playing to win and playing not to lose. Ask any NFL coach!

"WE LOST BECAUSE
WE TOLD OURSELVES
WE LOST."

LEO NIKOLAYEVICH TOLSTOY

THE WORST PROBLEM FOR ANY
MANAGER IS NOT RECOGNIZING
AND ACCEPTING THAT SHE
OR HE HAS A PROBLEM.

GOOD MANAGERS ARE
GOOD LISTENERS.
THEY ADHERE TO THE SUBTLE
LESSON OF NATURE—MAN HAS
TWO EARS AND ONE MOUTH.

"KNOW HOW TO LISTEN
AND YOU WILL PROFIT
EVEN FROM THOSE
WHO TALK BADLY."

PLUTARCH

THE LEADER'S JOB IS TO TEACH SO
THAT PEOPLE WILL KNOW, TO SHARE SO
PEOPLE WILL GROW, AND TO ENLIGHTEN
SO PEOPLE WILL HAVE HOPE.

"A LEADER IS A
DEALER IN HOPE."

NAPOLEON BONAPARTE

When your pupils become your teachers, you have reached management maturity.

It is a sad fact that the managers of the old are usually opponents of the new and that bottlenecks are almost always at the top of the bottle.

Management must accept the facts that the future will not simply be an extension of the past and the formulas that previously brought success will not continue to do so indefinitely.

Teamwork is not simply having everyone wear the same color shirt.

"TO SUCCEED AS A TEAM
IS TO HOLD ALL OF THE
MEMBERS ACCOUNTABLE
FOR THEIR EXPERTISE."

MITCHELL CAPLAN

SUCCESSFUL MANAGERS UNDERSTAND
AND ACCEPT THE FACT THAT THEY
CANNOT SOLVE TODAY'S PROBLEMS
WITH YESTERDAY'S SOLUTIONS.

"THE SIGNIFICANT
PROBLEMS WE FACE
CANNOT BE SOLVED AT
THE SAME LEVEL OF
THINKING WE WERE AT
WHEN WE CREATED THEM."

ALBERT EINSTEIN

ENTHUSIASM IS CONTAGIOUS.
THROUGH THE AGES IT HAS MOVED
MORE PEOPLE TO POSITIVE ACTION
THAN HAS RANK AND POSITION
OR COMMAND AND CONTROL.

"I RATE ENTHUSIASM
EVEN ABOVE
PROFESSIONAL SKILL."

SIR EDWARD APPLETON

When managers understand and accept that the functions and methods of management are being made obsolete by technology, competitors, and customers, they are on the road to transformation.

Managers must be willing to admit both publicly and to themselves that what they said yesterday was wrong.

"THERE IS A CERTAIN DEGREE OF SATISFACTION IN HAVING THE COURAGE TO ADMIT ONE'S ERRORS. IT NOT ONLY CLEARS UP THE AIR OF GUILT AND DEFENSIVENESS, BUT OFTEN HELPS SOLVE THE PROBLEM CREATED BY THE ERROR."

DALE CARNEGIE

IF YOU ALWAYS DO WHAT YOU'VE
ALWAYS DONE, YOU'LL ALWAYS
GET WHAT YOU'VE ALWAYS
GOTTEN—IF YOU'RE LUCKY!

Photo: Collection of the author

ON ORGANIZATIONS

Organization: A structure through which individuals cooperate systematically to conduct business.

Who could guess that just twenty-five years ago organizations actually operated with employees talking with and to each other? Managers were managing one-on-one, and leaders were teaching principles and values. Direct, face-to-face conversation was the way to communicate within the corporation, and the written memo was the guarantee that what was said was confirmed and appropriate action was to follow.

Fast forward twenty-five years, and organizations have replaced personal contact and teaching with e-mails and instant everything. The Internet god has demanded that we take no prisoners. Where have all the mentors gone within the organization? What is the process by which the organizational culture will be passed on to the next generation? How is all that we have learned in the past to be conveyed in a meaningful way? There is nothing wrong with progress as long as history and knowledge are not left to die by the side of the information superhighway. But this new, faceless environment does not easily allow employees to learn about managing, leading, valuing age-old principles, teaching, sharing, and caring. What's worse, people fail to know that they don't know! But I hope that, by putting some of this "wisdom" in writing, I will enable a few to read, comprehend, and learn.

THOSE ORGANIZATIONS THAT EMBRACE, RATHER THAN RESIST, CHANGE ALWAYS REACH THE FINISH LINE FIRST.

AN ORGANIZATION'S CULTURAL SHORTFALL IS THAT IT LINKS COMPANIES TO THE PAST, WHILE THE CHALLENGES LIE IN THE FUTURE. IT'S THE EQUIVALENT OF DRIVING THE EXPRESSWAY BY LOOKING IN THE REARVIEW MIRROR.

WHERE YOUR COMPANY HAS COME FROM IS LESS IMPORTANT THAN WHERE IT IS GOING.

"IN THE BUSINESS WORLD, THE REARVIEW MIRROR IS ALWAYS CLEARER THAN THE WINDSHIELD."

WARREN BUFFET

ORGANIZATIONS THAT OPERATE ON THE PREMISE THAT PRODUCT VOLUME ALWAYS FOLLOWS CONSUMPTION WILL ALWAYS OUTPERFORM THOSE THAT BELIEVE THE OPPOSITE.

AS BUSINESS ORGANIZATIONS BECOME MORE COMPLEX, THEY DEVELOP STRONG NATURAL TENDENCIES TO DRIFT AWAY FROM THEIR CUSTOMERS AS THEY SHIFT FROM AN EXTERNAL TO AN INTERNAL FOCUS.

ORGANIZATIONS MUST ENCOURAGE CROSS-FUNCTIONAL TEAMWORK AND CUSTOMER-SUPPLIER PARTNERSHIPS. THE OLD STOVEPIPE STRUCTURES WHERE VERTICAL COMMUNICATION WAS THE ORDER OF THE DAY ARE OBSOLETE AND SELF-DEFEATING.

IS WHAT YOU HAVE TODAY GOING TO GET YOU SUCCESSFULLY TO TOMORROW?

"EVERY ORGANIZATION IS PERFECTLY ALIGNED TO GET THE RESULTS IT GETS."

STEVEN COVEY

YOUR ORGANIZATION MUST BE PREPARED AND KNOW EXACTLY HOW IT WOULD BE AFFECTED AND WHAT STEPS IT MUST TAKE WERE ITS KEY CUSTOMER TO FORM A PARTNERSHIP WITH ITS KEY COMPETITOR TOMORROW.

DESPITE OVERWHELMING EVIDENCE, MOST ORGANIZATIONS ARE SURPRISED BY THE FACT THAT THE TRADITIONAL TWENTIETH-CENTURY BUSINESS MODEL IS DYING, AND THEY CONTINUE TO RELY ON SIMPLY DOING THINGS BETTER AS OPPOSED TO DOING THINGS DIFFERENTLY.

"IT IS PARDONABLE TO
BE DEFEATED BUT NEVER
TO BE SURPRISED."

FREDERICK THE GREAT

SUCCESS IS THE GREAT
ENEMY OF INNOVATION.

BUREAUCRACY IN ANY FORM
CRIPPLES AN ORGANIZATION.

YOU WILL NEVER ABANDON THE
PAST UNLESS YOU UNDERSTAND THE
OPPORTUNITIES FOR THE FUTURE.

"Most companies never knowingly recruit or hire a bureaucrat. Rather, management creates an environment where bureaucrats are allowed to grow and to flourish."

Edward E. Crutchfield Jr.

ORGANIZATIONS TYPICALLY HIRE
PEOPLE FOR THEIR STRENGTHS
AND THEN WASTE VALUABLE
TRAINING RESOURCES ADDRESSING
THEIR WEAKNESSES.

MOST ORGANIZATIONS SPEND 90
PERCENT OF THEIR TRAINING EFFORT
TEACHING PRODUCT KNOWLEDGE,
WHEN WHAT IS NEEDED MOST
IS CUSTOMER KNOWLEDGE.

MOST ORGANIZATIONS FAIL TO
REALIZE THAT COST REDUCTION
THROUGHOUT THE TOTAL SYSTEM
CAN MOST EFFICIENTLY BE
ACCOMPLISHED WHEN TRUST REPLACES
SKEPTICISM. TRUSTING SUPPLIERS,
CUSTOMERS, AND EMPLOYEES IS
ONE OF THE MOST EFFECTIVE,
YET UNDERUTILIZED, TECHNIQUES
AVAILABLE TO MANAGEMENT.

IF YOU THINK THAT SIMPLY DOING
MORE OF WHAT WORKED FOR YOUR
ORGANIZATION OVER THE LAST
TEN YEARS WILL BE ENOUGH TO
SUSTAIN GROWTH AND PROFITABILITY
FOR THE NEXT TEN, YOU HAVE
ALREADY LOST THE GAME.

"TO BE SUCCESSFUL, YOU HAVE TO BE ABLE TO RELATE TO PEOPLE; THEY HAVE TO BE SATISFIED WITH YOUR PERSONALITY TO BE ABLE TO DO BUSINESS WITH YOU AND TO BUILD A RELATIONSHIP WITH MUTUAL TRUST."

GEORGE ROSS

THERE IS NO SUCH THING AS INSTITUTIONAL MEMORY. THINK ABOUT IT—FIVE EMPLOYEES WITH A COMBINED WORK EXPERIENCE OF 150 YEARS RETIRE AND GET THEIR GOLD WATCHES, AND NOTHING THEY LEARNED OR CONTRIBUTED IS RECORDED OR PASSED ON TO FUTURE EMPLOYEES. THIS IS CORPORATE CRIME.

WHAT WILL SEPARATE THE TOP PERFORMING ORGANIZATIONS FROM ALL THE OTHERS WILL BE THEIR ABILITY TO CREATE, EXECUTE, AND SUSTAIN GENUINE LOVE AFFAIRS WITH THEIR SUPPLIERS, CUSTOMERS, AND EMPLOYEES.

MOST ORGANIZATIONS ARE 95 PERCENT PRODUCT AND MARKETING FOCUSED AND 5 PERCENT CUSTOMER FOCUSED, BUT PRODUCT AND MARKETING SUPERIORITY ALONE ARE NOT SUFFICIENT. CUSTOMER ALIGNMENT AND SYSTEMS SUPERIORITY ARE ESSENTIAL.

IN THE TWENTY-FIRST CENTURY, CHANGE WILL BE SO INTENSE AND SO TURBULENT THAT HURRICANE-WARNING FLAGS WILL BECOME PERMANENT FIXTURES.

"THE ART OF PROGRESS
IS TO PRESERVE ORDER
AMID CHANGE AND
CHANGE AMID ORDER."

ALFRED NORTH WHITEHEAD

MOST ORGANIZATIONS SEEK
COMFORT AND CERTAINTY, THE
VERY CONDITIONS MOST LIKELY TO
BRING ABOUT THEIR DECLINE.

THE FIRST SIGN THAT A COMPANY IS IN
TROUBLE IS WHEN ITS MANAGERS TELL
THEMSELVES HOW GOOD THE COMPANY
WAS IN THE PAST. WHEN MEMORIES
EXCEED DREAMS, THE END IS NEAR.

"A SHIP IN HARBOR
IS SAFE, BUT THAT
IS NOT WHAT SHIPS
ARE BUILT FOR."

WILLIAM SHEDD

TO REFORM MEANS HAVING PEOPLE DO
THE SAME THING MORE EFFICIENTLY.
TO TRANSFORM MEANS TO VIEW PEOPLE
IN A TOTALLY DIFFERENT LIGHT AND
USE THEM IN TOTALLY DIFFERENT WAYS.

"A CORPORATION IS A LIVING ORGANISM; IT HAS TO CONTINUE TO SHED ITS SKIN. METHODS HAVE TO CHANGE. VALUES HAVE TO CHANGE. THE SUM TOTAL OF THOSE CHANGES IS TRANSFORMATION."

ANDREW GROVE

Organizational structure and information systems, regardless of how sophisticated they are, must be totally (re)designed to link with those of a company's customers and suppliers at all key functional points.

Historically, successful organizations have always valued ideas over process.

An organization's products and services must be designed for meaningful differences rather than better sameness.

INNOVATIVE ORGANIZATIONS TAKE A QUANTUM LEAP OUT OF THE OLD SYSTEM, WHERE EVERYONE DOES BUSINESS THE SAME WAY. THEY TOTALLY CHANGE THE SYSTEM AND LEAVE THEIR COMPETITORS STRUGGLING TO WIN A GAME THAT THEY AND THEIR CUSTOMERS AND SUPPLIERS NO LONGER PLAY.

DIAGNOSING ALWAYS PRECEDES PRESCRIBING. PRESCRIBING WHAT YOU THINK THE CUSTOMER WANTS RATHER THAN DIAGNOSING WHAT THE CUSTOMER NEEDS IS CORPORATE ARROGANCE AND ALWAYS A FAILED STRATEGY.

"THIS MAY SEEM SIMPLE
BUT YOU NEED TO GIVE
CUSTOMERS WHAT THEY
WANT, NOT WHAT YOU
THINK THEY WANT. AND,
IF YOU DO THIS, PEOPLE
WILL KEEP COMING BACK."

JOHN ILHAN

In your haste to fix, have you ever learned how to build?

Simply creating and meeting product demand is no longer enough. Organizations must understand, then meet, then exceed the customer's needs, desires, and emotions—or remain forever locked in minor battles of incremental volume and profit loss and gain.

"WISE ARE THOSE WHO LEARN THAT THE BOTTOM LINE DOESN'T ALWAYS HAVE TO BE THEIR TOP PRIORITY."

WILLIAM A. WARD

THE EXCEPTIONAL ORGANIZATION
UNDERSTANDS THAT ITS FUNDAMENTAL
RESPONSIBILITY IS FIRST AND
FOREMOST TO THE CUSTOMER.

MOST ORGANIZATIONS WILL NOT
TOLERATE PROPHETS BECAUSE
PROPHETS DO NOT RESPECT RIGID AND
VENERABLE INSTITUTIONS; RATHER,
THEY VALUE IDEAS THAT OFTEN
INCLUDE THE INEVITABLE COLLAPSE
OF THE OLD ORGANIZATIONAL ORDER.

THE COMMAND AND CONTROL
MANAGEMENT STYLE IS A PRACTICE
WHERE THE TOP TELLS THE MIDDLE
TO DO "IT" TO THE BOTTOM—
AND "IT" IS FATALLY FLAWED.

FUSE THE DISTINCT CONCEPTS
AND PRACTICES OF LEADERSHIP
AND MANAGEMENT.

ORGANIZATIONS MUST ABOLISH
FUNCTIONAL FIEFDOMS THAT HAVE
THEIR OWN RULES, REGULATIONS,
AND VALUE SYSTEMS AND ARE
OFTEN NOT ALIGNED WITH THE
ORGANIZATION'S MISSION.

FEW ORGANIZATIONS FAIL BECAUSE
THEY HAVE THE WRONG ANSWERS.
MOST FAIL BECAUSE THEY DON'T ASK
THEMSELVES THE RIGHT QUESTIONS.

THE DIFFICULTY IN REINVENTING
ANY ORGANIZATION LIES NOT IN
DEVELOPING NEW IDEAS BUT IN
ESCAPING FROM THE OLD ONES.

THE NEW RULES AND NEW WAYS OF
DOING THINGS WILL ALWAYS BE WRITTEN
AT THE LONELY, FRAGILE, DANGEROUS,
FRIGHTENING EDGE—NEVER IN
THE COMFORT OF THE CENTER.

"'COME TO THE
EDGE,' HE SAID.
THEY SAID, 'WE ARE
AFRAID.' 'COME TO THE
EDGE,' HE SAID. THEY
CAME. HE PUSHED
THEM ... AND THEY FLEW.
THOSE WHO LOVE US MAY
WELL PUSH US WHEN
WE'RE READY TO FLY."

GUILLAUME APOLLINAIRE

BUREAUCRACIES FOCUS ON
REPLICATING SUCCESS VIA RIGID
ADHERENCE TO A COMPLEX SET OF
RULES, REGULATIONS, POLICIES,
PROCEDURES, SYSTEMS, AND
ORGANIZATIONAL STRUCTURES.
THEY AVOID IDEAS THAT DON'T FIT
INTO THEIR SUCCESS FORMULA, AND
THEY ARE SO ATTACHED TO THEIR
ESTABLISHED WAY OF BEING THAT
THEY FIND IT ALL BUT IMPOSSIBLE
TO RESPOND TO THE EVER-PRESENT
CHANGES IN THE MARKETPLACE.

"IN TIMES OF RAPID
CHANGE, EXPERIENCE
COULD BE YOUR
WORST ENEMY."

J. PAUL GETTY

Lou Pritchett, Barbara Pritchett, Helen Walton, and Sam Walton
Photo: Collection of the author

ON CUSTOMER PARTNERING

Partnering: A process of collaborative teamwork. It allows groups to achieve measurable results through agreements and productive working relationships. This process provides structure for teams to establish a mission by using common goals and shared objectives.

People often ask me where and when the "partnering concept" actually occurred to me as a viable business process. Although I didn't realize it at the time, I think it started when I was asked to deliver a keynote address to the 1982 annual meeting of the Philippine Association of Supermarkets (PASI). My main point was that I would insist that suppliers change the way they think about my operation. Rather than simply trying to sell me bigger orders, I would insist that they bring to me solid ideas which, when implemented, would automatically result in large orders. I would strongly advocate a *partnership* between us.

When I returned to the United States in 1984 as vice president of sales, I asked for a report that showed our largest customers and customers with whom we had major problems. When that report arrived, I was shocked to find that Wal-Mart headed both lists. I also learned that Wal-Mart management had never been visited by a corporate P&G officer. I decide to go see Mr. Sam Walton himself. This led to the now-famous canoe trip that was the genesis of the ultimate partnership between P&G and Wal-Mart.

It was on the river that we both came to realize that our two very large, complex, sophisticated companies were communicating with each other by essentially slipping notes under the door. We were each going our separate ways and doing nothing to add value to the process.

117

The only contact between these two multi-billion-dollar systems was a sales rep from P&G and a buyer from Wal-Mart, neither equipped to represent the total corporate system and each influenced by conflicting reward and recognition systems. We realized that we had several choices ranging from adversarial, where we currently were, to partnership, the ultimate win-win!

Sam and I agreed that, for both companies to not only survive into the 1990s but to prosper, we had to move from the short-term, adversarial, confrontational win-lose relationship that had been the hallmark of the previous twenty years to a partnership built on trust and committed to a shared vision. We had to work collaboratively to meet the consumers' needs while driving excess cost out of the system. We had to learn to work *on* the system instead of simply working *in* the system. Indeed, we had to change the system, together. We realized that we were plowing new ground. Therefore, like Thomas Edison—who didn't invent the lightbulb by tinkering with the candle—we had to start with a fresh sheet of paper, take risks, and think outside the box.

THE OBJECTIVE OF THE CUSTOMER-SUPPLIER PARTNERSHIP IS TO CREATE AND SUSTAIN A MUTUALLY PRODUCTIVE RELATIONSHIP IN WHICH BOTH PARTIES' NEEDS ARE MET SHORT- AND LONG-TERM. TOO MANY MANAGERS BELIEVE THE OBJECTIVE SIMPLY TO BE BETTER TRADE RELATIONS IN THE HOPES OF MORE SHORT-TERM VOLUME.

"YOUR MOST UNHAPPY
CUSTOMERS ARE YOUR
GREATEST SOURCE
OF LEARNING."

BILL GATES

CUSTOMERS ARE LOYAL TO A
PRODUCT ONLY UNTIL WHICH TIME
THEY DISCOVER SOMETHING BETTER.
THE CONCEPT OF CUSTOMER
LOYALTY IS HIGHLY DEBATABLE.

"CONSUMERS ARE
STATISTICS. CUSTOMERS
ARE PEOPLE."

STANLEY MARCUS

CUSTOMERS AND SUPPLIERS MUST OPERATE AS EXTENSIONS OF EACH OTHER'S OPERATIONS. HOW EFFECTIVE WOULD IT BE IF EVERY MORNING, EACH WOULD ARISE AND ASK, "WHAT DO MY CUSTOMERS/ SUPPLIERS NEED FROM ME TODAY?"

"THERE IS ONLY ONE BOSS: THE CUSTOMER. AND HE CAN FIRE EVERYBODY IN THE COMPANY FROM THE CHAIRMAN ON DOWN, SIMPLY BY SPENDING HIS MONEY SOMEWHERE ELSE."

SAM WALTON

THE PRIMARY JOB OF A SALES
ORGANIZATION IS TO REPRESENT
THE CUSTOMER TO THE COMPANY—
NOT THE OTHER WAY AROUND.

TO DRAMATICALLY ENHANCE OPEN
COMMUNICATION AND REENERGIZE
THE ENTIRE ORGANIZATION, THE
TRADITIONAL PYRAMID ORGANIZATIONAL
STRUCTURE MUST BE FLATTENED
TO ELIMINATE STRUCTURAL LAYERS
AND INTERNAL-FUNCTION WALLS.

THE HISTORICAL PRACTICE OF
INDIVIDUALS FOCUSING ON AND
MANAGING THEIR OWN CAREER
PATHS MUST GIVE WAY TO A NEW
SENSE OF COOPERATION AND
TEAMWORK, WHERE THE INDIVIDUAL
WINS ONLY WHEN THE TEAM WINS.

REALIZE THAT HELPING OTHERS
GET WHAT THEY WANT IS THE
SUREST AND FASTEST WAY OF
GETTING WHAT YOU WANT.

"THE MAGIC FORMULA THAT
SUCCESSFUL BUSINESSES
HAVE DISCOVERED IS TO
TREAT CUSTOMERS LIKE
GUESTS AND EMPLOYEES
LIKE PEOPLE."

TOM PETERS

ACCEPT THAT PEOPLE, SYSTEMS,
AND SERVICE—NOT PRODUCTS—WILL
SUSTAIN A SUCCESSFUL ENTERPRISE.

PEOPLE DO OR DON'T DO WHAT
THEY ARE REWARDED, RECOGNIZED,
OR PUNISHED FOR DOING OR NOT
DOING. THEREFORE, CHOOSE TO
CAREFULLY MEASURE AND REWARD
THAT WHICH YOU WANT TO ACHIEVE.

CHOOSE TO WORK MULTI-FUNCTIONALLY:
CREATE TEAMS AND DEMAND LATERAL
AS WELL AS VERTICAL COMMUNICATION.

SUCCESS ULTIMATELY COMES
DOWN TO TAKING CARE OF YOUR
EMPLOYEES AND CUSTOMERS BETTER
THAN YOUR COMPETITORS DO.

CHOOSE TO WORK ON THE TOTAL
SYSTEM: EXTERNAL ALIGNMENT,
INTERNAL ALIGNMENT, AND
ORGANIZATIONAL CAPACITY (MAKE
SURE THAT YOUR PEOPLE CAN
DELIVER ON YOUR COMMITMENT).
AVOID TRYING TO FIX THE PIECES.

CHOOSE TO ACCEPT THAT THE
SOONER YOU REALIZE THAT YOU
ARE BEHIND, THE MORE TIME
YOU WILL HAVE TO CATCH UP.

"TIME IS THE SCARCEST
RESOURCE, AND UNLESS
IT IS MANAGED, NOTHING
ELSE CAN BE MANAGED."

PETER DRUCKER

NEVER PARTNER WITH A CUSTOMER
OR SUPPLIER IF YOU CANNOT OR
WILL NOT MEASURE THE RESULTS.

CHOOSE FIRST TO FOCUS ON THE
CUSTOMER RATHER THAN ON YOUR
OWN INTERNAL OPERATION.

"THE MOST IMPORTANT
ADAGE AND THE ONLY
ADAGE IS, THE CUSTOMER
COMES FIRST; WHATEVER
THE BUSINESS, THE
CUSTOMER COMES FIRST."

KERRY STOKES

CORPORATE MANAGEMENT MUST UNDERSTAND THAT EXPERTISE TODAY RESIDES IN THE END-USING CUSTOMER AND THAT THE REAL EXPERTS ON ANY PRODUCT OR SERVICE DO NOT WORK FOR THE COMPANY—THEY ARE THE COMPANY'S CUSTOMERS! CHOOSE TO ASSESS THE CUSTOMER'S NEEDS; THEN MOVE FROM RELIABILITY TO FLEXIBILITY TO INNOVATION.

"WE SEE OUR CUSTOMERS AS INVITED GUESTS TO A PARTY, AND WE ARE THE HOSTS. IT'S OUR JOB EVERY DAY TO MAKE EVERY IMPORTANT ASPECT OF THE CUSTOMER EXPERIENCE A LITTLE BIT BETTER."

JEFF BEZOS

CHOOSE TO INVEST THE RESOURCES,
TOOLS, AND TRAINING TO GET THE
RESULTS BOTH PARTNERS DESIRE.
THERE IS NO RETURN WITHOUT AN
INVESTMENT; MAKE THE INVESTMENT
BEFORE YOU ARE FORCED TO. YOU
CANNOT INVEST ONLY WHAT YOU
HAVE ON HAND AND WON'T MISS;
BOTH PARTNERS MUST ACCEPT
AND COMMIT TO INVESTING.

CHOOSE TO LET GO OF TODAY'S
TRAPEZE IN ORDER TO GRAB
TOMORROW'S; DON'T GET
CAUGHT IN BETWEEN.

"IT'S NOT SO MUCH THAT
WE'RE AFRAID OF CHANGE
OR SO IN LOVE WITH
THE OLD WAYS, BUT IT'S
THAT PLACE IN BETWEEN
THAT WE FEAR. IT'S
LIKE BEING IN BETWEEN
TRAPEZES. IT'S LINUS
WHEN HIS BLANKET IS
IN THE DRYER. THERE'S
NOTHING TO HOLD ON TO."

MARILYN FERGUSON

You must constantly ask yourself what you want to do for your customers in three to five years that you cannot do for them today.

Corporate downsizing must be replaced by rightsizing. Downsizing is a losing cost-reduction strategy. Rightsizing is not a euphemism; it means having the right people at the right place with the right tools at the right time.

Accept that the status quo isn't. In organizations, as with nature, if something isn't growing, it's dying.

"EVERYTHING IS IN A
CONSTANT STATE OF
CHANGE. NOTHING EVER
STAYS THE SAME."

HERACLITUS

CUSTOMER-SUPPLIER PARTNERSHIPS
AND STRATEGIC ALIGNMENTS
BUILT ON TRUST MUST REPLACE
CONFRONTATIONAL WIN-
LOSE RELATIONSHIPS.

"You only win if you aren't afraid to lose."

Rocky Aoki

CORPORATE INTERNAL FUNCTIONS,
WITH THEIR OWN IDIOSYNCRATIC RULES,
REGULATIONS, SYSTEMS, VALUES, AND
HIERARCHIES, MUST BE REPLACED
BY MULTI-FUNCTIONAL TEAMS.

"LIFE IS ONE INDIVISIBLE WHOLE. ONE CANNOT DO RIGHT IN ONE DEPARTMENT OF LIFE WHILST HE IS OCCUPIED IN DOING WRONG IN ANY OTHER DEPARTMENT."

MAHATMA GANDHI

TODAY'S CUSTOMER WANTS THE SUPPLIER TO HELP CONSERVE TIME; THE GIFT OF TIME MUST BECOME AN INTEGRAL PART OF THE ADDED VALUE OF YOUR PRODUCT OR SERVICE BECAUSE THE GIFT OF TIME IS, IN REALITY, THE GIFT OF MONEY.

"TIME IS THE COIN OF YOUR LIFE. IT IS THE ONLY COIN YOU HAVE, AND ONLY YOU CAN DETERMINE HOW IT WILL BE SPENT. BE CAREFUL LEST YOU LET OTHER PEOPLE SPEND IT FOR YOU."

CARL SANDBURG

THE FACT THAT YOUR COMPANY IS
MULTIDIVISIONAL, MULTIFUNCTIONAL,
MULTIREGIONAL, MULTIPLANT,
AND MULTIPRODUCT IS NOT
YOUR CUSTOMER'S PROBLEM.

THE FIRST LESSON IN SELLING
IS, MAKE IT EASY FOR THE BUYER
TO BUY. ALWAYS GIVE BUYERS
A CHOICE BETWEEN SOMETHING
AND SOMETHING, NEVER BETWEEN
SOMETHING AND NOTHING.

"MAKE YOUR PRODUCT
EASIER TO BUY THAN
YOUR COMPETITION'S
OR YOU WILL FIND YOUR
CUSTOMERS BUYING
FROM THEM, NOT YOU."

MARK CUBAN

AN ORGANIZATION THAT TAKES
AN UNDIFFERENTIATED APPROACH
TO SERVING ITS CUSTOMERS BY
TREATING ALL OF THEM THE SAME
WAY WILL TREAT ITS BEST CUSTOMERS
LIKE ITS WORST ONES AND ITS
WORST ONES LIKE ITS BEST.

MANAGING THE SUPPLY CHAIN,
FROM SUPPLIER TO CUSTOMER TO
CONSUMER, ENABLED BY INFORMATION
TECHNOLOGY, IS EVERY BIT AS
IMPORTANT AS MANAGING BRANDS.

Photo Credit: Rob Kaufman

On People

In the twenty-first century, raw materials and technology will be available to every company in every country in the world. Therefore, the only thing that will separate the winners from the losers will be the quality, character training, and commitment of an empowered workforce. I am constantly amazed at the number of managers, at all levels, who fail to understand this most basic principle. This new recognition about the individual has nothing to do with being nice to people; it is simply a realization that people will either make or break your company.

Only when you begin to treat people as partner/owners will you begin to reap the full benefits of what an organization can do. Only when management forms psychological contracts with employees will there be 100 percent commitment. And the key is to trust them, because people can never be trustworthy until they experience the overt act of first being trusted. My observation over the years has been that the most successful managers have not necessarily been those with the best business skills; rather, they have been those with the most finely-honed people skills—those who have been able to get ordinary people to do extraordinary things. Of course, you must really believe in the power and potential of people. You cannot just give it lip service or pretend to believe it. You must feel it in your soul twenty-four hours a day, every day. Once you experience the results of this mindset, you will realize that operating any other way places you and your organization at a distinct competitive disadvantage.

Please do not be confused by the word "ordinary." This word is used in the most positive way to describe people of character who know they have character; people who are willing to pay a price in terms of hard work and personal sacrifice to attain their goals; people who respect others and are willing to go the extra mile for the good of the whole. These ordinary people are the same ones who plowed our fields, dug our mines, built our cities, pushed our national boundaries from the Atlantic to the Pacific, fought our wars, and paid our taxes. They are ordinary only in the sense that they are the ones who collectively answer the call, rise to the occasion, and serve without fanfare. These ordinary people are found in every corporation and at every level in American business, and they do those extraordinary things that make companies successful when management does what it gets paid to do—provide leadership and the proper workplace environment.

Fortunately for management, people want to participate in helping plan and build their companies for the future. Therefore, one of the most intelligent things that good business leaders do is give their people the choice of becoming architects or bricklayers in building new models for their organizations. Given a choice, my experience has been that the majority will choose to become architects, and this is good, for it will be a most dangerous time for business when men and women stop wanting to participate in the design process. When maintaining the status quo replaces the desire to challenge, experiment, question, and change, we have seen the end of productive enterprise. However, harnessing this talent requires that management provide the environment and take overt action to ensure that each person in the organization is offered the opportunity to decide if he or she wants to be a servant of what *is* or a shaper of what *might be*.

The bottom line on people is quite simple: if you don't want to be forever locked in a repetitive battle of profit and loss and a costly cycle of training and retraining, avoid the mistake of undervaluing your employees. Realize that the *skillful* deployment of the human resource is the single most important task facing management.

Performance must replace conformity as the benchmark for employee value. Conformity limits freedom of expression. Performance is open ended.

Entrepreneurship (looking outward, taking risks) must be valued over stewardship (looking inward, preserving corporate assets).

"YOU MISS 100
PERCENT OF THE SHOTS
YOU NEVER TAKE."

WAYNE GRETZKY

Human resources must be viewed not as costs to be reduced whenever and wherever possible but as assets requiring maintenance and investment.

In the new global economy, raw materials and technology will be available to every company in every country in the world. Only people will be unique in the system.

One of the best-kept secrets in business is that each and every employee, regardless of rank, is a unique source of knowledge. When management learns how to fully capitalize on this knowledge, it will have reached nirvana.

"THE PARADOX OF
OUR TIMES IS THAT WE
ARE INUNDATED WITH
INFORMATION YET STARVED
FOR KNOWLEDGE."

WILLIAM R. BRADY

PEOPLE ARE WHAT MAKE OR BREAK
A COMPANY. WE ALL AGREE THAT A
SPORTS TEAM IS NO BETTER THAN
THE MEMBERS WHO MAKE IT UP.
THEN WHY DO WE NOT BELIEVE THE
SAME IS TRUE FOR A COMPANY?

"THE GREAT LEADERS
ARE LIKE THE BEST
CONDUCTORS—THEY
REACH BEYOND THE
NOTES TO REACH THE
MAGIC IN THE PLAYERS."

BLAINE LEE

DEPLOYING THE HUMAN RESOURCE
PROPERLY IS THE GENIUS OF
GOOD MANAGEMENT.

"EVERY SUCCESSFUL
ENTERPRISE REQUIRES
THREE MEN: A DREAMER,
A BUSINESSMAN, AND
A SON-OF-A-BITCH."

PETER MCARTHUR

THE HUMAN RESOURCE IS
FAR MORE VALUABLE THAN
THE CAPITAL RESOURCE.
UNFORTUNATELY, WE NEVER SEE THIS
MEASURED ON THE BALANCE SHEET.

"PEOPLE ARE DEFINITELY A COMPANY'S GREATEST ASSET. IT DOESN'T MAKE ANY DIFFERENCE WHETHER THE PRODUCT IS CARS OR COSMETICS. A COMPANY IS ONLY AS GOOD AS THE PEOPLE IT KEEPS."

MARY KAY ASH

THE REAL VALUE TO COMPANIES IN THE UNFORGIVING FUTURE WILL NOT BE MANAGERS WHO TEACH PEOPLE TO EXECUTE, IT WILL BE LEADERS WHO TEACH PEOPLE TO DREAM. YOU MUST MAKE ROOM FOR DREAMERS AND POETS BECAUSE AN IDEA IS A THOUSAND TIMES MORE POWERFUL THAN A FACT, AND IDEAS ARE THE NEW CURRENCY IN THE TWENTY-FIRST CENTURY.

"A MAN MAY DIE, NATIONS MAY RISE AND FALL, BUT AN IDEA LIVES ON."

JOHN F. KENNEDY

CUSTOMIZED TRAINING DESIGNED TO
GIVE EACH INDIVIDUAL THE TOOLS
HE OR SHE NEEDS MUST REPLACE
GENERIC, MASS-ORIENTED PROGRAMS.

WHEN MANAGEMENT THINKS OF
PEOPLE MERELY AS "BACKS AND
BRAWN," IT FAILS TO TAP THE
MOST POWERFUL OF ALL FORCES:
BRAINS AND HUMAN SPIRIT.

"COMPUTERS ARE
MAGNIFICENT TOOLS FOR
THE REALIZATION OF
OUR DREAMS, BUT NO
MACHINE CAN REPLACE
THE HUMAN SPARK OF
SPIRIT, COMPASSION, LOVE,
AND UNDERSTANDING."

LOUIS GERSTNER

Make room for "industrial priests," those committed individuals who deeply believe in a better way, are emotionally committed to finding it, and are willing to suffer the pain of leading change.

"LIFE IS CHANGE.
GROWTH IS OPTIONAL.
CHOOSE WISELY."

ANONYMOUS

Human beings do not get up in the morning and decide to go to work and screw up! This being true, why do so many managers think they must manage via command and control?

Most organizations fail to accept that people tend to support best that which they help create. This failure results in grossly underutilizing human resources.

To reach 100 percent customer satisfaction, you must have reached 100 percent employee satisfaction. Human beings will make or break a company!

> "HUMAN RELATIONSHIPS
> ARE THE KEY TO
> ALL COMMERCE."
>
> ROBYN ALLEN

THERE IS NO SUCH THING AS A
GREAT CUSTOMER COMPANY THAT IS
NOT A GREAT PEOPLE COMPANY.

BEFORE YOU BLAME YOUR PEOPLE
FOR YOUR ORGANIZATION'S
SHORTCOMINGS, CONSIDER THAT
MOST OF THEM HAVE BECOME
EXPERTS WITHIN A LOUSY SYSTEM.

"THE PEOPLE WHO WORK
IN CORPORATIONS ARE NOT
THE PROBLEM. IT IS THE
SYSTEMS AND STRUCTURES
IN WHICH THEY WORK THAT
CREATE THE PROBLEMS."

W. EDWARDS DEMING

PEOPLE ARE FREQUENTLY MISJUDGED
BY THEIR SUPERIORS BUT NEVER
BY THEIR SUBORDINATES.

EACH INDIVIDUAL CAN CHOOSE
WHETHER TO BE A BRICKLAYER OR
AN ARCHITECT. IN THE BUSINESS
CONTEXT, BRICKLAYERS RUN
BUSINESSES; ARCHITECTS BUILD THEM.

THE ENTIRE WORKFORCE SHOULD
BE ENCOURAGED, IF NOT REQUIRED,
TO THINK OUTSIDE THE BOX AND
TO CHALLENGE ALL THE RULES,
REGULATIONS AND CONTROLS IN
ORDER TO FIND A BETTER WAY.

PEOPLE TEND TO BECOME THAT
WHICH THEY THINK OTHERS THINK
THEY ARE. IF YOU THINK OF THEM AS
LOSERS, THEY WILL BECOME LOSERS.
IF YOU THINK OF THEM AS WINNERS
THEY WILL BECOME WINNERS.

"THE WAY YOU SEE THEM
IS THE WAY YOU TREAT
THEM, AND THE WAY
YOU TREAT THEM IS THE
WAY THEY BECOME."

ZIG ZIGLAR

"LEADERSHIP GEOMETRY" IS BRINGING
THE VERY BEST OUT OF PEOPLE
BY FIRST TRUSTING THEM, THEN
DEPLOYING THEM PROPERLY, AND
THEN ALLOWING THEM TO PARTICIPATE
BEYOND THEIR JOB DESCRIPTIONS.
THIS IS BASED ON THE PRINCIPLE
THAT PEOPLE TEND TO SUPPORT BEST
THAT WHICH THEY HELP CREATE.

"TELL ME AND I WILL
FORGET. SHOW ME
AND I WILL REMEMBER.
INVOLVE ME AND I
WILL UNDERSTAND."

CONFUCIUS

Management must understand that the human workforce is the single most expensive and important asset it has—and must commit to investing in its care and well-being, including improved health care, family, and training needs. Learning must become the company's competitive edge.

"GREAT THINGS HAVE
BEEN EFFECTED BY A FEW
MEN WELL CONDUCTED."

GEORGE ROGERS CLARK

Photo: Collection of the author

ON TECHNOLOGY

Technology: Human innovation in action that involves the generation of knowledge and processes to develop systems that solve problems and extend human capabilities.

My good friend, author and speaker Jim Harris, always informs his clients that he cannot tell anyone what the future will look like, but he *can* tell everyone that it will not look like the present or the past.

I heard a very bright futurist tell an audience that he found it fascinating that for the past hundred years, scholars, intellectuals, writers, professors, and even cartoonists had predicted that by the year 2000, we would have television, wrist radios, helicopters, interstate highways linking the great cities, travel to the moon, and deep space exploration. However, not one single person predicted the Internet and World Wide Web and the linking, via computers, of people to people, people to business, and business to business.

I am now in my seventies and will make no effort to lecture you about this new and fascinating technology. The one point I do want to emphasize, however, is the absolute necessity of staying cutting-edge. While Sam Walton and I were hammering out the P&G/Wal-Mart partnership, one of the major driving points was our belief that by working together and bringing our systems into alignment, we could drive excess costs out of the system. That was the early 1980s, and we of course knew nothing about the incredible breakthroughs in communications technology that were not too far around the corner. But we were both confident that technology was changing and changing rapidly—and knew that we had to be prepared to embrace new developments faster and more efficiently than our competitors. So we utilized the existing technology to the maximum degree possible, always recognizing that we had to be prepared to let it go to grab the technology of tomorrow at a moment's notice. However impressed you may be with today's state of the art, realize that you will be thinking of it as quaint within five years, and that we truly haven't seen anything yet.

Although I am extremely reluctant to make any predictions as to the fate of any existing business in this new e-world, I am willing to say that, to succeed, all businesses must shift from their historic focus on problem solving to a new focus of opportunity seeing. The future will belong to those individuals with imagination in seizing opportunities, not in trying to optimize solutions, and to companies that are physically, mentally, emotionally, and electronically aligned with the customer.

Finally, although I can't recall who said it, in fewer than fifty words this sage summed up precisely what I have tried to communicate in this book: *Although this new network economy is founded on technology, it can only be built on relationships. Although it all starts with chips, it had better end with trust, and trust can only be established through personal contact—one human being to another.*

ENABLED BY INFORMATION
TECHNOLOGY, THE REPLACEMENT
OF CONFRONTATION AND SECRECY
WITH COOPERATION AND SHARED
INFORMATION WILL BE THE COST
OF ENTRY FOR DOING BUSINESS IN
THE TWENTY-FIRST CENTURY.

"IN THIS NEW WAVE OF
TECHNOLOGY, YOU CAN'T
DO IT ALL YOURSELF, YOU
HAVE TO FORM ALLIANCES."

CARLOS SLIM HELU

INFORMATION TECHNOLOGY WILL DRIVE CHANGE IN THE TWENTY-FIRST CENTURY JUST AS SURELY AS MANUFACTURING DROVE IT IN THE TWENTIETH. THEREFORE, SUCCESS IN THE TWENTY-FIRST CENTURY WILL DEPEND ON ACCESS TO INFORMATION, NOT ACCESS TO CAPITAL.

"TECHNOLOGY IS A WAY OF
ORGANIZING THE UNIVERSE
SO THAT MAN DOESN'T
HAVE TO EXPERIENCE IT."

MAX FRISCH

COMPANIES WHICH CONTINUE
A TRADITIONAL "WE SELL, YOU
BUY" RELATIONSHIP WITH THEIR
CUSTOMERS WILL FIND THEMSELVES
INCREASINGLY OBSOLETE IN THE
TWENTY-FIRST CENTURY.

"HUMANITY IS ACQUIRING ALL THE RIGHT TECHNOLOGY FOR ALL THE WRONG REASONS."

R. BUCKMINSTER FULLER

Given that they now have immediate access to nearly all data, workers must now be granted— and accept—full responsibility for total participation in the business process. They can neither be forced nor allowed to sit back and wait for the boss to tell them what to do. Each individual must become proactive, which requires not only doing but also thinking.

"ROTATING PEOPLE AND LETTING THEM WORK IN DIFFERENT ASSIGNMENTS IS AN EXCELLENT WAY TO KEEP A PERSON'S WORK INTERESTING. IT SERVES TO ENRICH AND DEVELOP THE EMPLOYEE'S SKILLS. IT'S A PITY THAT IT ISN'T PRACTICED MORE WIDELY."

ANDY GROVE

IN THIS HIGH-SPEED INTERNET WORLD, WHEN THE RATE OF EXTERNAL CHANGE EXCEEDS THE RATE OF INTERNAL CHANGE, DISASTER IS IMMINENT!

"THE POLICY OF BEING
TOO CAUTIOUS IS THE
GREATEST RISK OF ALL."

JAWAHARLAL NEHRU

THE HALLMARK OF ALL SUCCESSFUL
PEOPLE IS THAT THEY ANTICIPATE
CHANGE, WELCOME IT, AND ARE
ALWAYS THE FIRST TO ACCEPT
IT AND CAPITALIZE ON IT.

"GENTLEMEN, IF YOU WANT
TO SUCCEED, YOU MUST
ALWAYS RIDE TOWARD
THE SOUND OF BATTLE."

"STONEWALL" JACKSON

INFORMATION TECHNOLOGY HAS CONNECTED US MORE CLOSELY WITH OUR CUSTOMERS, SUPPLIERS AND EMPLOYEES THAN EVER BEFORE IN HISTORY. UNFORTUNATELY, IT HAS ALSO LEFT US FEELING MORE DISCONNECTED THAN EVER BEFORE IN HISTORY.

IN THIS NEW INFORMATION AGE, WE WILL HAVE WITHIN THE ORGANIZATION MORE EXPERT TECHNICIANS THAN EXPERIENCED MANAGERS. WITH THIS COMES A LOSS OF SKILLS IN MANAGING THE KEY COMPONENTS OF ANY BUSINESS: EMPLOYEES, CUSTOMERS, AND SUPPLIERS.

"THERE ARE MANAGERS SO PREOCCUPIED WITH THEIR E-MAIL MESSAGES THAT THEY NEVER LOOK UP FROM THEIR SCREENS TO SEE WHAT'S HAPPENING IN THE NON-DIGITAL WORLD."

MIHALY CSIKSZENTMIHALYI

IN TODAY'S CORPORATE WORLD, FORGIVENESS IS EASIER TO OBTAIN THAN PERMISSION. SIMPLY DO IT!

"IF COLUMBUS HAD AN
ADVISORY COMMITTEE,
HE WOULD PROBABLY
STILL BE AT THE DOCK."

ARTHUR J. GOLDBERG

BECOME A CHANGE AGENT WITHIN YOUR ORGANIZATION, BUT ALWAYS REMEMBER THE CHANGE AGENT'S CARDINAL RULE: NEVER SACRIFICE YOURSELF ON THE FIELD OF BATTLE, RATHER LIVE TO FIGHT ANOTHER DAY.

CHANGING THE ORDER OF THINGS WILL REQUIRE LEAVING BEHIND SOME OF THOSE THINGS THAT ONCE SERVED US WELL BUT NOW HOLD US BACK. THIS WILL DEMAND AS MUCH UNLEARNING AS IT WILL LEARNING.

"THE ILLITERATE OF THE TWENTY-FIRST CENTURY WILL NOT BE THOSE WHO CANNOT READ AND WRITE BUT THOSE WHO CANNOT LEARN, UNLEARN, AND RELEARN."

ALVIN TOFFLER

Photo Credit: Rob Kaufman

PARTING THOUGHTS

As I stated in the introduction of this book, my original objective was to summarize much of the learning I had gleaned from teachers, subordinates, peers, superiors, and writers during my long business career and to find a way to caution my readers that they can't rely solely on the Internet for this material. As I began to assemble and put this material on paper, it also became clear to me that I was actually trying to do something else: I was trying to send a wake-up call that would send people off into the future fully armed with universal truth and ageless wisdom.

Quite honestly, I was surprised at how determined and committed I felt to giving aid and comfort to today's young men and women who are wed to things electronic—not necessarily by choice, but rather by fiat—and who just may have missed the last great age of learning through the up-close–and-personal caring and sharing of one human being to another. Today's young people are not unlike those of previous generations, people who have been called movers, shakers, change agents, entrepreneurs, and just plain weirdos. These are the men and women from all walks of life who are never satisfied with the status quo, who are always uncomfortable with just a job, who are always asking "what if?," and who are deeply depressed during the lull between finishing a project and starting a new one. These are the individuals who honestly feel that if they aren't stretching, pushing, and challenging the system and everybody in it, they aren't earning their pay. These are the men and women who thoroughly enjoy taking on city hall or senior management because they, like Thomas Jefferson, know that there is a better way and they are driven to help find it. These are individuals who do not suffer fools lightly, who innately know that those with rank are handicapped by that very rank. They are the people I call the "boat rockers," and throughout history they have been the ones who have made the difference in politics, in education, in religion, in the military, in business, and in society in general.

Unfortunately, for many "boat paddlers," boat rockers make life very uncomfortable. They create unwanted motion, they make waves, they speed up events, they change the direction of the boat, and, in the process, they make the paddlers seasick. Sadly, the captains of the ships in which many of the rockers are riding demand that they sit down, shut up, and just paddle like all the others. These captains want no conflict, no rough water, no counter motion to the speed and direction they are steering the ship. Few of these captains and paddlers recognize that the very safety and success of the ship is created by the people they want to silence.

Therefore, readers, I suggest that you continue to rock the boat and encourage your boat captain to quickly learn to recognize and encourage you to rock even harder because, in this take no prisoners information- and knowledge-driven era of ours, it is the paddlers who are the threat to the enterprise and it is the rockers who will save it.

ABOUT THE AUTHOR

Lou Pritchett grew up in Memphis, Tennessee and graduated from the University of Memphis in 1953. He immediately joined the Procter & Gamble Company as a soap salesman in Tupelo, Mississippi. In 1957, he went on active duty with the US Army, but soon returned to P&G, where he rose through the ranks, serving in a number of management positions including division sales manager, president of the company's Philippine subsidiary, headquartered in Manila, and corporate vice president, sales, where he was instrumental in the creation of the now-famous partnership between P&G and Wal-Mart. Upon retiring in 1989, Lou started his own public-speaking business and spent several years traveling the United States and the world, speaking to business organizations about customer/supplier relationships. His first book, *Stop Paddling & Start Rocking the Boat* was published in 1995, and is now in its fourth printing. In 1999, Lou was awarded the Distinguished Eagle Scout Award. Lou is now retired with his wife, Barbara, in Ponte Vedra Beach, Florida.